BOOK 4

THE MANUAL

ATTITUDE/GRATITUDE/
PROPER FOOD

CARL BEECH WITH
MATT BIRD
AND STEVE MARTIN

BIOGS

Carl

Matt

Steve

Carl is married to Karen and has two daughters. He's the leader of CVM (an international men's movement) and the founder of 'the code'. Previously a banker, church planter and senior pastor, he is convinced he is a great chef, plays the piano, loves cycling, movies and sci-fi books and caught a record-breaking catfish on the river Ebro in Spain.
Twitter @carlfbeech

Matt Bird is the CEO of Make It* Happen, which creates value for leaders and organisations by helping them build the relationships they need in order to achieve greater success. He has created a new social science, Relationology.

Steve spent 28 years in the Royal Navy, runs the Naval Christian Fellowship, works for CVM, has a beard, plays the guitar, runs marathons, is married with two sons, and wants blokes to get to know and follow Jesus.

Copyright © Carl Beech 2012
Published 2012 by CWR, Waverley Abbey House, Waverley Lane, Farnham,
Surrey GU9 8EP, UK.
Registered Charity No. 294387. Registered Limited Company No. 1990308.
The rights of Carl Beech, Matt Bird and Steve Martin to be identified as the authors of
this work have been asserted by them in accordance with the Copyright, Designs and
Patents Act 1988.
For a list of National Distributors visit www.cwr.org.uk/distributors
Unless otherwise indicated, all Scripture references are from the Holy Bible:
New International Version (NIV), copyright © 1973, 1978, 1984, 2011 by Biblica
(formerly the International Bible Society).
Other versions used: *The Message*: Scripture taken from *The Message*.
Copyright © 1993, 1994, 1995, 1996, 2000, 2001, 2002. Used by permission of
NavPress Publishing Group.
Concept development, editing, design and production by CWR
Printed in Croatia by Zrinski
ISBN: 978-1-85345-886-6

Contents

BOOK 4

[INTRO]

We've finally cracked it!
After being asked to write daily
notes for men a number of times
over the years, we've finally
nailed it. So, in a nutshell, here
you go and let the journey begin!

It's a simple and well-proven
approach. The notes are between
150–300 words long. Each day
begins with a verse and ends in a
prayer. It will take you no more than
a few minutes to read but I hope
that what you read stays in your
head throughout your day. The
notes are numbered rather than
dated, so it's OK if you miss a day to
pick it back up. If you want to study
with a group of guys you can easily
keep track of where you are up to
or swap ideas on that particular
study online (we've a Facebook
page). If you want to be part of a
band of brothers internationally
swapping thoughts, insights and
prayer requests then you can
do that as well by using our new
Facebook page.

In each issue, I've asked some of my mates to contribute. In this one, big thanks go to Matt Bird and Steve Martin for their insights and thoughts. They're gunning for God and have some great things to say. We really hope that the subjects from Attitude to Proper Food speak into all our lives and help us stay on the narrow path.

So there it is. The Word of God has such power to inform and transform our lives, so let's knuckle down and get reading.

Your brother in Christ
Carl

[IT'S ALL ABOUT TIMING]

01/Seasons

'There is a time for everything, and a season for every activity under the heavens.' **Ecclesiastes 3:1**

One of the major flaws of activists is that they want to do everything yesterday. Another is that they tend to work only at one speed: full on! I know this because I am one. However, there is great wisdom in recognising, as a man, that life runs in seasons. I was talking to a guy the other day who was reminiscing about a past period of his life. It soon became clear to me that he was still living in those days, even though in reality life had moved on. That was then, I wanted to tell him, this is now! It struck me that we can so easily miss out on what God is doing because we are harking back to an earlier season. What's more, we can miss out on what He is wanting to do now because we crowd it out with other stuff and don't stop to listen, or pause to realise that things are different now.

What I do find hysterical is the way we always view the past through a pair of rose-tinted spectacles that Elton John would be proud of. I remember an old *Alas Smith and Jones* sketch where one of them was playing the part of a posh MP. 'An old lady came up to me the other day and said, "Why oh why can't it be like the old days?" So I took away her pension and shoved her grandson up the chimney.' Good point well made, I thought.

So, remember that there are seasons in life. Enjoy today but be prepared to move on tomorrow and don't spend too much time looking back and wasting the moment you are in right now.

Prayer: Thank You, God, for the seasons in life. There are good times and bad times, ups and downs, challenges and times when it's easier. Thank You that all of this is part of life. Amen.

02/ Death and life

'A time to be born and a time to die ...'
Ecclesiastes 3:2

Are you ready to die? Seriously. If you were called to account for your life today, would you be ready? Who would you need to have made peace with? What regrets would you have? What have you not done yet that you would have wanted to see done in your lifetime?

It's a fact that we will all die. I will, you will, everyone you know will. I don't think it's a bad thing to think about that as a follower of Jesus. I think about it. I know that I don't have any rehearsal time and, if I want my life to count for something, I need to seize the day and crack on. And I don't think it's depressing to think about death either, especially as someone who knows his eternal destiny. Frankly, the prospect of dying should in some ways be exciting. I get that the process of dying may not exactly float your boat but, at the end of the day, for us who follow Jesus, it's no bad thing. And for those who haven't decided yet, why not seize the day and do it?

Whatever your situation, you don't want to die with regrets. So, take this today as an encouragement to make some decisions. Make peace with someone. Ask for forgiveness where necessary. Tell that mate about Jesus. Say to your family what you've always wanted to say deep down but haven't, because 'I'm a bloke and blokes don't share their feelings ...' Resolve to get done what you heard God ask you to do years ago and never did. We've only got one shot and we don't know how long it'll last. Make it count!

Prayer: Give me a sharp edge to my life that makes every day count. Give me a passion for life so that I make the most of every opportunity. Give me the grace to go through life at peace with people. Make me determined to serve You well. Amen.

03/Break it down!

> 'A time to tear down and a time to build ...' **Ecclesiastes 3:3**

Tricky one, this – but it's worth seriously pondering on. It's so hard to stop doing something when it seems to be working. It's incredibly tough to come to a decision that something you have laboured over, poured time, energy and money into, has had its day. But the fact is that so often we find it hard to stop doing stuff, only to then watch it slowly decline because in reality it has served its purpose.

Now, don't take this as some 'prophetic word' that what you are doing has had its day – I'm not saying that. What I *am* saying, however, is that closing stuff down isn't something that comes easy to Christians. Or to men, come to that. We hate to admit defeat and we hate to fail, and we would rather grind ourselves into the ground than do either. It is, however, a biblical principle to call time on something and actively dismantle stuff. So, ask questions about some of the things you are involved in, particularly kingdom activities.

Why are you doing them? Because you always have? Why are certain things done the way they are? Because they've always been done that way? If that's your answer, perhaps it's time to have a serious think.

Here are some questions I put to churches: Why are meetings always on Wednesdays? Why do we always worship first, then get a preach? Why do we only talk about the incarnation at Christmas? Why do we have organ music? Why do we drink tea out of green cups and saucers at church but nowhere else? So many questions, so few answers! Sometimes we just need to change stuff because we're stuck in a rut bigger than the one I left when I tried to drive my car onto the beach ...

Prayer: Help me to be analytical and honest about the things I'm doing. Give me courage to stop and courage to tear down when it's right to. Amen.

04/Crying shame

'A time to weep and a time to laugh ...'
Ecclesiastes 3:4

We were designed to cry, I've no doubt about that. We also have the ability to keep a stiff upper lip when required – no doubt about that, either. The trick, it seems to me, is to allow yourself to 'let it out' and show emotion when you need to but also to know when you need to 'wind it in a bit' for the sake of those around you. Sometimes as men we need to be strong for people; at other times they need to see us cry and show vulnerability. In fact, my daughters told me the other day they had never seen me cry. I was a bit surprised by that, so I asked them if they had ever seen me laugh uncontrollably. Apparently they had seen me do that. I realise now that there is a side to me I haven't let them see, and I need to deal with that and show them that Dad has feelings, too. (Just don't expect me to cry at *Little House on the Prairie* – there are limits!)

Now, I have got mates who cry at chick flicks, but for the most part they don't let their guards down nearly enough. So, why do men find it hard to cry? Perhaps we've been brought up not to. Perhaps we think it's not manly. Maybe we are afraid that if we do, people will think we're weak. Frankly, all of those reasons are a bit rubbish, really. So, here's a thought for today: Let people see you laugh, let them see you cry. Take the risk of being vulnerable in front of your family and friends. Allow people to see the real you that's under the surface.

If we do that, life may feel just a little bit different. As people see the real us, it may even lead to deeper relationships.

Prayer: Give me the strength to be vulnerable, the heart to be honest and the grit to cry. Amen.

05/Shut it!

'A time to be silent and a time to speak ...' **Ecclesiastes 3:7**

Sometimes you find yourself talking to a guy who has the answer to what you are saying before you've even finished saying what you're trying to say. As a result, he gives you an answer to only part of your point, which only means you have to explain it all over again. A bloke like that is really annoying! Equally annoying is when you are talking to someone and they don't look at you because they're distracted by their phone or the TV or someone else. (I'm guilty of that one.)

Men aren't always good listeners. We tune out easily, we always have an answer and we seem to be experts on everything. Take, for example, a recent visit to the pub. It was shortly after the discovery of the Higgs boson and there were two Derbyshire lads talking very animatedly about the possibility of travelling faster than the speed of light because 'there are no G-forces'. Do me a favour!

We all need to learn to be less of an expert and more of a listener. The amazing thing is that once you start to take time to listen to people, not only do you start to learn stuff but the people you've been listening to walk away thinking they've had a brilliant conversation! Funny but very true. Get a reputation for listening to people and tuning in to what they are saying, not a reputation for being a know-all who never listens.

Prayer: Show me when to speak and when to listen. Help me to bite my tongue and not leap in at the first opportunity. Help me to be secure enough to let other people have their say. Amen.

An inability to stay quiet is one of the most conspicuous failings of mankind.
WALTER BAGEHOT

[TEN BLISTERING
COMMANDMENTS]

06/God alone

'You shall have no other gods
before me.' **Exodus 20:3**

This is the first of the Ten Commandments and
it's preceded by a verse that says that it was
God who rescued His people and no other deity.
There were lots of man-made gods competing for
people's attention in those days. The Canaanites
had dozens of 'em and the Egyptians maybe had
over a hundred. The Israelites were unique in that
they worshipped only one: God. However, there
was always a very real danger that they might
lose it on that one. So, God wanted to nail this
issue right at the start of the Commandments.
It was from this understanding that all the other
Commandments flowed.

So, what does this mean for us today? You'd be
making a mistake if you thought it wasn't relevant
to us. The world is becoming very tolerant of
freedom of choice, but highly *in*tolerant of what it
regards as intolerance. Say that 'Jesus is the only
way' and it can easily cause offence. There can be

huge pressure to yield and simply say 'perhaps we are all worshipping the same Being anyway.' But that's not true and there's no place for that kind of thinking for those of us who follow Jesus. Sometimes we need to remember that. Don't be on the back foot when you talk about your faith. Yes, we should listen to people and not be belligerent. Yes, we should enter into dialogue with people of other faiths and beliefs. But we should never give way on the truth that Jesus is the only way.

If that does cause offence we just need to man up and go through the pain barrier.

Prayer: I declare today that there is only one God. I reaffirm before You, God, that Jesus alone provides the way to heaven. Strengthen my belief and my resolve and guard me from diluting my faith. Amen.

07/Idols

'You shall not make for yourself
an image in the form of anything
in heaven above or on the earth
beneath or in the waters below.'
Exodus 20:4

I used to have a Fireblade. That's a superbly
engineered, seriously fast and totally cool-looking
motorbike for those who don't know. In fact, over
the years I've owned a number of bikes. I was
never into Harley-Davidsons, though – I don't
think a bike is a bike unless it looks like a UFO and
does 0–60 in under four seconds.

I haven't had a bike for the last three years,
however. Let me explain why. I was tooling round
some country lanes when I nearly got wiped out
by a car coming round the bend towards me on
the wrong side of the road. That in itself was not a
problem – near misses happen. The problem was
my reaction. I realised that I was more worried
about the bike than my body. I knew this because
as the car roared past me, my first thought was

how much it would cost to repair the bike if it got hit! I also discovered that when my wife suggested it was time to give it all up, the thought of not having a bike was totally gutting. In other words, it had become an idol. It had to go.

Of course, in Old Testament times there were other forms of idols: statues, fetishes, images, all depicting gods of man's imagining. We may not have that issue to deal with today, but we do create other forms of idolatry. God is a jealous God and He wants absolute priority in our lives – the trouble is that us guys so often and so easily develop idols. It could be fitness, success, work, music, anything. Maybe we need to make an honest assessment of our priorities and take any action required.

Prayer: May You be first in my life, God. Test my heart and show me if I am putting anything before You and my relationship with You. Amen.

08/Blasphemy

'You shall not misuse the name of the LORD your God, for the LORD will not hold anyone guiltless who misuses his name.' **Exodus 20:7**

I'm sure you've asked this question before. Why is it that the name 'Jesus' is used almost universally as a swear word and yet you never hear people using 'Mohammed', 'Krishna' or 'Siddhartha Guatama' in the same way? Why is it that people who don't even believe in Him exclaim 'Jesus Christ!' when they're trying to make a point, or sigh 'Oh God ...'? Strange, isn't it?

I guess that one answer is that the name of Jesus is hugely powerful. We know from Acts 19 that the use of the name 'Jesus' got a reaction from evil spirits. We also know that, according to John 14:13-14, whatever we ask for in the name of Jesus will be given to us.

Let's think about this for a moment and dig a bit deeper. Are there other, less obvious ways in which we might be misusing God's name? How about saying stuff like 'As God is my Judge, I swear ...'? You know the kind of thing. Jesus told us to let our 'Yes' mean 'Yes' and our 'No' mean 'No'. He told us not to swear oaths using God's name. Taking it a bit further, how about when we say: 'Well, God told me ...' or 'God gave that idea to me ...'? It's very hard to argue with someone who talks like that! More to the point, if you're going to make such a claim you'd better be very sure you are absolutely convinced it's true.

The bottom line is this: us men should be uttering the name of God in awe and reverence. Anything less than that and we're possibly heading into Exodus 20:7 territory.

Prayer: Father, I determine to hold Your name in honour and respect. I will not misuse it – and I won't make bold statements and use Your name to back them up inappropriately. Amen.

09/Sabbath

'Remember the Sabbath day by keeping it holy.' **Exodus 20:8**

The Pharisees (the most religious people in Jesus' day) had some strange ways of keeping the Sabbath holy. They invented a huge number of rules and regulations. For example, they said you couldn't tie a knot, except in a woman's girdle – so the only way to get water from the well was to tie the bucket to a girdle and the girdle to a rope! In fact, there were 39 types of work you couldn't do on the Sabbath, including preparing food (which is why, in Matthew 12, some of them had a go at Jesus for picking corn). They even had a go at Him for healing people (see Mark 3:1-6). Crazy stuff!

That is not what this is all about. We need to get to the heart of this Commandment or we will end up laying heavy burdens on ourselves, just like the Pharisees did. In essence, it means we should have a day set apart (which is what 'holy' means) when we remember God in a focused way: we stop doing the work that earns us our bread and butter and we devote some time to worship, prayer and learning more about Him.

I like the idea of doing that in community. I've always noticed how people hang around at my church after the meeting. Perhaps we should make more of an effort to eat with people on the Sabbath, laugh together and 'do life' together as well as engage with God more. Whenever I can I make sure that I go to a church meeting with my family, but it's also a time to spend with other believers and create a dynamic where it's easy to talk about God and share the stuff we see Him doing. That's what it means to me to keep the Sabbath holy: it's about God and it's about people.

Prayer: Help me to make the most of one day each week to be with other people and engage with You. Forgive me for the times I haven't made the Sabbath a priority. Amen.

10/Respect!

'Honour your father and your mother, so that you may live long in the land the LORD your God is giving you.' **Exodus 20:12**

This is the only one of the Commandments that comes with a spin-off benefit! As I write this, I'm fully aware that some blokes who read this may have lost both of their parents. Others may not even have known their mum and dad, or perhaps have had very little contact with them. But let's look at the principle here of giving honour. It seems to me that we're not so good at honouring leaders or elders (both outside and within the Church). We seem to have a culture which talks more about rights and entitlements than about duties and responsibilities, and one in which it's very easy to attack the boss and disrespect older people.

OK, rant over. Let's consider what honouring someone looks like in practice. Does it mean doing everything they say without question, or bowing and scraping in their presence? Of course not. That would be crazy and not helpful to anyone, including the person on the receiving end. Instead, it means that we don't indulge in criticism or gossip about them. It means trying our best to make life easier for them and giving them the benefit of the doubt when we feel a bit miffed. It also means talking to them with respect and showing them a bit of intelligent deference.

For those of us with a parent or two, it may look a little different; but the same principle applies. It means listening, even when we think we know best (at any age and stage), showing patience and respect. It means being attentive. If Simon Cowell can phone his mum every day, I'm sure we can all make a good go of it!

Prayer: I pray today for my parents/mentors/overseers/ leaders/bosses. I pray for their happiness, strength and wisdom. Give me a heart that is open to learn from them and help me to show them respect and honour. Amen.

11/Murder

'You shall not murder.' **Exodus 20:13**

It seems pretty obvious to us but maybe it wasn't at the time it was written. Imagine hundreds of thousands of people in convoy traipsing through the desert in the Exodus. You can imagine the feuds and skirmishes that must have broken out between individuals, families and clans. I'm sure it could have been hugely tempting, as well as quite easy, to bump someone off and hide them behind a cactus. So, a commandment was issued, and it's one that has filtered through the legal systems of established societies throughout the world. Still today, murder is regarded as one of the most heinous of crimes. The taking of a life without just cause has been for millennia condemned as murder, and in some societies it can mean you forfeit your own life.

As ever, however, Jesus takes it a little bit further. Murder, like all sin, He says, begins in the human heart (Mark 7:20–23). It starts as a thought – hate, maybe, or greed (see James 1:13–15; 4:1–3) – which eventually results in death. On the other hand, the total opposite of hating someone is loving them, not seeking revenge but looking for ways to help them out (Rom. 12:17–21). More than that: according to Matthew 5:21–22, you get angry, you're subject to judgment. So, seriously ponder on this, fellas. Carry hate in your heart and it's as if you're committing murder. Surely that can't be right, can it?

Prayer: Keep hatred from my heart and help me, as far as it is possible, to live at peace with people. Amen.

Anger is a killing thing: it kills the man who angers, for each rage leaves him less than he had been before – it takes something from him.

LOUIS L'AMOUR

12/Playing away

'You shall not commit adultery.'
Exodus 20:14

When David went for a wander on a balcony one evening and clapped eyes on Bathsheba (2 Sam. 11), it wasn't long before he had jumped into bed with her and arranged for her husband to be bumped off. I've often pondered on this story. How did that happen? Was it a one-off stroll on the balcony or had David been taking the odd diversion for a 'cheeky look' over a period of time? That's the thing with the 'sin thing': it starts with a wrong turning and before you know it, it has taken you down a path you didn't want to travel and you end up in a place you really don't like! Matthew 7 talks about staying on the narrow path and there's a reason for that. A plane flying thousands of miles needs only to go a degree or two off course to end up many miles from where it should be at the end of the journey. Similarly, it can take only a small deviation from the narrow path to end up in a hell of a place.

Again, Jesus takes this further and puts His finger on the source of the problem. Lust after a woman, He says, and you've already committed adultery in your heart (Matt. 5:27–28). Ouch! So, chaps, it's eyes front, keep your powder dry and your trousers on. And let's avoid balcony time we know we shouldn't be taking. It's not an easy fight, but it's crucial we take our stand.

Prayer: Keep my heart pure and free from lust. Keep my eyes from wandering and my thought life free from sin. Amen.

If a man has no opportunity of living with another man's wife, but ... would do so if he could, he is no less guilty than if he was caught in the act.

SAINT AUGUSTINE

13/Thieving monkey

'You shall not steal.' **Exodus 20:15**

Stealing can mean much more than nicking a bit of pick 'n' mix. Let's have a ponder about it. How about offering to pay your builder cash 'to avoid the VAT'? For some, that's debatable, of course, because it's not your problem, is it, if he doesn't pay his tax. How about stealing time from your employer, or using work resources for personal business? What about not letting on when you've been given too much change? How about overclaiming expenses or nicking some petty cash? I could go on and on and on, I guess.

We do tend to categorise sin on a sliding scale. There's epic stealing, like a bank job, and there's corporate fraud such as raiding pension funds or inflating profits. The recent banking crisis – largely caused by greed – nearly wrecked the world economy, to an extent that is hard for us to comprehend. Most of us will never go to such extremes, but dishonesty easily creeps in. Take the recent scandal in the UK of MPs' expense claims, for which a few went 'inside'.

I guess that greed is always going to be a major driver for theft of all shapes and sizes – facilitated by a numbed and blunted conscience. It's about integrity, really. Generally speaking, the Holy Spirit is easily grieved and He very quickly pricks your conscience when you've crossed a line. For us guys, it's about hearing His quiet objection to our actions and then nipping our dishonesty in the bud.

Prayer: Father, stop me in my tracks when my actions are anything less than honourable. Help me to hear and recognise Your voice when I am straying too close to the line. Amen.

14/False

'You shall not give false testimony against your neighbour.' **Exodus 20:16**

In court they call this 'perjury'. Tell a lie under oath and they'll throw the book at you. Solomon warned that false witnesses will not go unpunished (Prov. 19:5). Jesus also said that what comes out of a man's mouth can defile him (Matt. 15:11). Not good, then!

Now, this Commandment focuses on giving false testimony in court but let's think about speaking untruths generally and the impact that it can have on our lives. Personally, I think that habitual lying can pretty much drive you mad. I've known a few guys who lied so much they forgot what was true and what was false. But why do we lie? To cover our tracks, maybe? Perhaps to enhance a story to make it or us sound better. Others make things up because it's just too painful to admit the truth. I guess there are all manner of reasons. A colleague of mine used to work with someone who seemed to live in a total fantasy land – they lied about their relationships, their holidays, their money, everything! My colleague put it down to loneliness and a huge inferiority complex, and I'm sure that *is* why some people tell falsehoods.

The problem, of course, is that lies lead to more lies and then more lies. Not good at all, and very stressful! I mean, how do you keep up with what the truth is and what you have said to who? That's when you end up living in a fantasy land. So, here's the solution. If the truth seems too painful to admit, man up, grit your teeth and take the pain. And if the source of the pain is that your life feels devoid of worth and lying makes things seem more interesting, get some good men around you, be honest with them about where you are at, meditate on Romans 8:15 and discover where your true identity is.

Prayer: Help me to be a man of truth and not lies, of facts and not fiction. Amen.

15/Greedy

'You shall not covet.' **Exodus 20:17**

The verse goes on to list things that men, in particular, seem to covet: women, cars (or oxen in those days) and basically anything your neighbour has that you don't! They used to call it 'keeping up with the Joneses', but these days the buzzword is 'consumerism'. We want it all now – and I mean *all* and I mean *now*. Payment options, credit cards, loans and finance schemes are all out there to entice us to purchase the previously unpurchasable. Not even the financial crisis seems to have dampened down personal consumerism. Last month alone, I had so many loan offers emailed or posted to me I could have got nearly a quarter of a million pounds. Crazy!

J.D. Rockefeller, the richest man of his day and (adjusting for inflation) possibly the richest man ever, was once asked how much money it took to be truly happy. His reply was 'Just a little bit more!' Ain't that the truth? Enough is never enough, it seems, when it comes to this stuff. It's our sinful nature that is to blame, and the law of diminishing returns. That's why the Bible constantly urges us to lead a simple life and not worry about possessions.

I'm aware that some of us are really under pressure, maybe struggling under the weight of having to pay back loans. If that is you, why not give our friends at Christians Against Poverty (CAP) a ring? In any event, let's get a grip on our consumerism and learn to be content with the simple things. If you find yourself coveting something, try waiting a week or two before you buy it. You'll usually find the desire goes – and with the money you save you could take someone you love out for a meal!

Prayer: Protect my heart from greed and the forces of consumerism. Help me to be content with the simple pleasures in life. Help me to regain a sense of perspective. _[If you are in debt:]_ Please give me the wisdom, self-discipline, guidance and help I need to free myself from debt over the next few years. Amen.

16/The fear factor

'Moses said to the people, "Do not be afraid. God has come to test you, so that the fear of God will be with you to keep you from sinning."'
Exodus 20:20

Moses had been up the mountain to receive the Ten Commandments. When he told the Israelites what God had said, it's an understatement to say that the people were scared out of their wits. There was a massive pyrotechnic display with added thunderclouds and a prevailing sense of doom. In fact, we know that God even told them not to come up the mountainside because they would wind up dead! So traumatised were they that they begged Moses to talk to God at a distance and stop Him speaking to them (Exod. 20:18-19).

Moses' answer is intriguing. Basically, he said that they had nothing to fear but, all the same, God was reminding them that it was worth noting just how powerful and awesome He is, so that they didn't sin! So many times we hear teaching which says that the reason we don't sin is because of our love for God and His love for us. H'mm. I guess that is true but that's not always as motivational as the fear of being wiped out by a thunderbolt! I have to be clear on this: I really do think we have lost a healthy sense of the fear of God. We've overdosed on fluff and forgotten about His power, majesty and glory. Our songs speak of Jesus more in terms of some kind of mildly erotic 'bromance' than as our Rescuer and Captain. It's all got a bit out of balance. So, take note: God uses our fear of Him to motivate us to stay on the straight and narrow. Yes, I know we are 'post cross and resurrection' and all that – but it's still the same God we are talking about.

As the noted Bible teacher R.T. Kendall once asked: Is your God too nice ...?

Prayer: Father, give me a better sense of Your power, majesty and glory. Develop in me a healthy fear of You – not a fear that paralyses relationship but one that is based on awe, respect and honour. Amen.

[PHILIPPIANS]

17/Thanks a million

'I thank my God every time I
remember you. In all my prayers
for all of you, I always pray with joy
because of your partnership in the
gospel from the first day until now ...'
Philippians 1:3-5

What a way to start a letter! In fact, all 104
verses that make up this book overflow with
the language of gratitude. OK, to be fair, that's
probably because it was a response to some gift
the apostle Paul had received from the church
at Philippi! Nonetheless, we can take some
good stuff from this. I wonder, if we audited our
conversations, what would be the ratio of praise
and thankfulness to moaning and complaining?
I tell you what, over the years I've found you get a
much better response from people if you start by
expressing your thanks!

By sheer coincidence, I had just started writing
this when I had to go to a meeting in the local pub
with the chairman of CVM, and some bloke was

in there moaning his head off to a young waitress in front of everyone. It just sounded awful. Now, I totally get it that there's a place for kicking up a stink about something or putting a complaint in, but usually that's got to be a last resort. It's far better to try to resolve things in a positive way. It's amazing the difference it can make when you change the way you go about things. It's biblical, too – Philippians 2:14 being a notable instance you can quickly flick to.

Prayer: Keep thanks and praise in my thoughts and on my lips, and not moaning and complaining. May I be a man known more for gratitude than a lack of it. Amen.

18/Finish well!

'... being confident of this, that he who began a good work in you will carry it on to completion until the day of Christ Jesus.' **Philippians 1:6**

The fact is that we're in a marathon, not a sprint. Too many men live their Christian lives as though we are in a 100-metre dash with Usain Bolt. The end result is inevitably disappointment, and sometimes they even give up on the things of God for a while – or even forever. In several places, the Bible says that walking (never mind running!) with Jesus is about enduring to the end and finishing strongly. Paul's hope here is that the Lord, who started a work in you and me, will see us through to the very end. Note he's not saying that He will – which is a debate for another time – he is expressing the *hope*. It's an important distinction to make, because the potential is there for casualties during the marathon race which we call 'discipleship'.

When I ran an actual marathon a couple of years ago, I couldn't believe the pace of all the other runners at the start. It totally threw me – I thought I was going to come last! Of course, after eight miles or so I began to recognise people who had overtaken me earlier as I started to go past them. This is what we do with our walk of faith. Sometimes we mistakenly turn it into a run. We go to a festival or a conference and get all fired up, only to hit the wall when we get back. Or we launch ourselves into a dozen church projects, only to burn out a year down the line. We're in this for the long haul, however, and it needs long-haul pacing. Sure, there are seasons when you will be manically busy, but build in the time for rest too, and spiritual disciplines that will keep you close to God to the end.

Prayer: Help me to run so as to finish strongly. Show me where I need to pace myself better in life. Amen.

19/Chain reaction

'Now I want you to know, brothers and sisters, that what has happened to me has actually served to advance the gospel. As a result, it has become clear throughout the whole palace guard and to everyone else that I am in chains for Christ. And because of my chains, most of the brothers and sisters have become confident in the Lord and dare all the more to proclaim the gospel without fear.'
Philippians 1:12-14

Imagine having to guard the apostle Paul. I bet he never shut up about Jesus! Even though he was facing a possible death sentence, his focus was on sharing the gospel. I love that. No matter the pressure of circumstances, he was driven by a passion to make Jesus known and to see even his jailers, who might end up killing him, transformed by the good news. And it had a spin-off effect. The people who were close to Paul in Rome (where he wrote this letter from prison) saw him in action, saw his commitment, his drive and his lack of fear and started to get stuck in themselves.

You know what, it's no different for us. The way we live, the way we conduct ourselves, the way we share our faith, the language we use, the opportunities we take or waste – I could go on – have a massive impact on the people around us. If you are a man of prayer, there's a good chance that your family will be prayerful, too. If you are a guy who shares his faith, there's a good chance that other people will follow your example in some way. I'm sure you get the point. We know that Paul was not a physically attractive bloke, but his passion for Jesus was so infectious that it touched those around him. Let's be the same!

Prayer: May my words, my actions and my attitude inspire people to follow You fearlessly and make You known. Amen.

20/Live or die?

'For to me, to live is Christ and to die is gain. If I am to go on living in the body, this will mean fruitful labour for me. Yet what shall I choose? I do not know! I am torn between the two: I desire to depart and be with Christ, which is better by far ...' Philippians 1:21-23

I remember, a few years ago, for a couple of days I had a really strange feeling in my gut. It wasn't the effects of a late-night kebab, I hasten to add, more a kind of homesickness. It was a bit weird, really, considering I was at home with my family. Finally, I found myself sitting in an armchair asking God what was wrong with me. The answer has stayed with me to this day: deep inside, I had a sense that I was feeling homesick because I wasn't truly home yet. The fact is that this life will end. I will die and you will die, and when that day comes and we breathe our last breaths, those of us who know Jesus will instantly find ourselves with Him. We will be home at last and we will be truly alive.

In many senses, full and real life is yet to come. Paul knows this and that's why he seems to be struggling here. He wants to live but he also wants to be with Jesus. In fact, he goes on to say that his only motivation for staying alive is to complete the work God has given him to do! Amazing, really.

I think it's important for us men, who can so easily be distracted by the things of this world, to remember that 'to live is Christ but to die is gain.' Can we truly say that? Is that where we're at? Or do we need a rethink?

Prayer: Help me really to understand what it means to say 'To live is Christ, to die is gain.' Help me to make life decisions that are focused more on the gospel than the things of this world. Amen.

[RELATIONOLOGY]

21/No man is an island

'God created mankind in his own image ...' **Genesis 1:27**

It is sobering to think that God has created man to be like Him (though not the same as Him). God creates, man creates. God works, man works. God rests, man rests. God battles, man battles. God provides, man provides. God protects, man protects. God sacrifices, man sacrifices. God loves, man loves.

At the very heart of God is relationship. The Father loves the Son and the Son loves the Father; the Father sent the Son into the world, and now the Father and the Son together send the Spirit into the world. The Trinity is both mysterious and scientifically logical – God is three: $1 + 1 + 1 = 3$ and God is also one: $1 \times 1 \times 1 = 1$. God exists in an interdependent community of relationships based on love, self-giving and sacrifice. Man is created to be like God, and so is born for relationship – and that's what I call 'relationology'.

We are most human when we are in healthy relationship with other people. Anything else is a denial of our God-given humanity and identity. Relationships determine how happy our lives are (think for a moment what it's like going to work when you've just fallen out with your wife!), our impact on society (strong family relationships build good neighbourhood relationships) and our success at work (the true currency of business is relationships, not money). No man is an island.

Who are your most important relationships with – and why?

Prayer: God, help me to be a man who builds healthy relationships in my home, my neighbourhood and my workplace. Amen.

22/Superhumans are human too

'In the spring, at the time when kings go off to war, David ... remained in Jerusalem.' **2 Samuel 11:1**

There is a potent lesson for men in the story of David and Bathsheba. While other kings went off to war, David stayed at home and from his rooftop terrace one evening he saw this rather stunning woman having a bath. He invited her over, they slept together and she became pregnant. Next, David arranged for her husband, Uriah, to come home from the war, hoping that he would sleep with her and everyone would assume that her baby was his. However, Uriah didn't sleep with his wife, so as a last resort David sent him back to the front and ordered his commander to make sure he died in battle. Bathsheba mourned her husband, and then David married her!

His first mistake wasn't seducing Bathsheba or even taking pleasure in gazing at her body from his rooftop. His first mistake was allowing himself to become isolated from his relationships with other men. He sent his army off to war but, unlike other kings, he remained at home. It doesn't matter who we are or what we have achieved, we are all vulnerable – even kings. Superhumans are human, too!

I remember a preacher once saying: 'Sin will take you where you do not want to go and will cost you more than you are willing to pay.' That was certainly the case for David. What friendships do you need to invest in to help keep yourself pure and faithful?

Prayer: God, help me to work hard to keep out of trouble. Help me to stick close to my friends and save me from going to places where I am vulnerable. Amen.

23/Be friendly

'While Jesus was having dinner at Matthew's house, many tax collectors and sinners came and ate with him and his disciples.' **Matthew 9:10**

Jesus invited a dozen men He called 'disciples' to join Him in His campaign. Among them, He had three core friends, Peter, James and John, who He took with Him into the most private situations – like when He went to a garden called Gethsemane to pray to His Father (Mark 14:33). He was especially close to John, who is described several times as 'the disciple whom Jesus loved' (eg John 13:23). His wider circle also included 'tax collectors and sinners' – for which the religious people despised Him – and, beyond that, He was followed by crowds in their hundreds and sometimes their thousands. Jesus had both a few intimate friends and great numbers of people He was friendly with.

One of my 'relationology' principles is: You can't be friends with everybody but you can be friendly to everybody. None of us can befriend everyone we know in the same way, but that doesn't stop us being friendly to everyone. Friendliness is something we need to practise. It is easy being friendly to someone who we think may be useful to us, but more important is how we treat someone we think *can't* really help us. For friendliness to be really authentic, we need to show it to everyone, including bus drivers, checkout assistants and waiters as well as our CEO and our MP.

What do you need to change in yourself to become a more friendly person today?

_____

Prayer: God, please help me to be the best friend I possibly can be to my friends and to be genuinely friendly to everyone else, including total strangers. Amen.

_____

24/Give to grow

'Even the Son of Man did not come to be served, but to serve, and to give his life as a ransom for many.'
Mark 10:45

Isn't that just amazing, that the King of kings comes to earth and does not want to be treated as such? I love the way that some of the churches I visit have a 'protocol team' who will carry my Bible for me, and any bags I have with me, and escort me throughout my visit and fetch water and refreshments for me, and then run me home afterwards, no matter how far I have travelled – it is incredible to be honoured in this way! And yet Jesus came to run a protocol team Himself to escort people into the kingdom of God ...

I once heard somebody talk about an approach to relationships they described as 'give to get'. They explained that in order to get something out of a relationship, you first need to put something into it. I know what they meant – and yet there is something about it that makes me feel uncomfortable. So, I have developed an alternative, 'relationology' approach which I now champion: 'give to grow'. This is about putting something into a relationship so that its long-term value will grow, rather than just to get short-term gain.

How can you serve the people you know today? How can you put something into your relationships today in a way that grows them for the long term?

_____

Prayer: God, please help me to serve You and serve the people I know. Guard me from being a consumer of You and a consumer of other people. Amen.

_____

25/Blind spot

'On a Sabbath Jesus was teaching
in one of the synagogues, and a
woman was there who had been
crippled by a spirit for eighteen
years. She was bent over and could
not straighten up at all. When Jesus
saw her, he called her forward
and said to her, "Woman, you
are set free from your infirmity."
Then he put his hands on her,
and immediately she straightened
up and praised God. Indignant
because Jesus had healed on the
Sabbath, the synagogue leader said
to the people, "There are six days
for work. So come and be healed on
those days, not on the Sabbath."'
Luke 13:10-14

Talk about missing the point! Here we have an
outstanding miracle, a long-term, debilitating
physical condition totally healed right in front of
the people, and all this guy can think of is that

it was done on the wrong day of the week! No sense of awe or compassion, just an obsession with rules and regulations.

We can fall into the same error ourselves. I was in a church once where a stand-up row broke out between the pastor and a member of the leadership about the coffee. I kid you not! I've been in a meeting at a church that had baptised nine people the previous Sunday and that night, an angry debate erupted over some minor repair work that needed doing.

It's all about spiritual blind spots. Jesus draws attention to them time and again in the Gospels. So, what are we more worked up about, the church budget or whether the poor are being cared for and people are being saved? Are we more concerned with 'doing things properly' or with proclaiming and demonstrating the gospel? And it's not just about church life, either – we can be Pharisees at work and at home. The 'religious' mindset so easily takes hold of us. Keep an eye out for it!

Prayer: Make me less of a Pharisee and more of a can-do, will-do kind of man, who sees the real priorities.

26/English or Dijon?

'Then Jesus asked, "What is the kingdom of God like? What shall I compare it to? It is like a mustard seed, which a man took and planted in his garden. It grew and became a tree, and the birds perched in its branches."' **Luke 13:18-19**

Never underestimate the effect of your activities for Jesus. That throwaway comment, that refusal to compromise your integrity, that demonstration of radically different values to people around you – all can have a massive impact. What I've discovered is this: as a follower of Jesus, you shape the culture around you. Let me explain. In your place of work, if you hold the line when it comes to your language, you will find that people start to moderate their language around you. Maybe not everyone and maybe not straightaway, but over time it will happen. Gradually, as you refuse to compromise (albeit in a joyful and gracious manner), you'll find that the spiritual climate there begins to change.

I have a mate who had to make some people redundant but did it in such a mind-blowingly gracious way that it changed the culture in his office long-term. There is now a Christian Union there that is totally thriving. The thing is that his character and his bearing up to that point had also been distinctly different and so, when the opportunity came, he demonstrated the values of the gospel and it was credible. He even told the assembled office how his faith had helped him in times past when he himself had faced redundancy. People have come to Christ there as a result of his ministry.

It's the mustard-seed effect. Don't underestimate the impact of small things. They take root and they grow!

Prayer: Give me a mustard-seed ministry where I live and work, and let me see it grow into something powerful for the gospel. Help me to spot opportunities to be an influence, even in small ways, for Your kingdom. Amen.

27/About giving ...

'As Jesus looked up, he saw the rich putting their gifts into the temple treasury. He also saw a poor widow put in two very small copper coins. "Truly I tell you," he said, "this poor widow has put in more than all the others. All these people gave their gifts out of their wealth; but she out of her poverty put in all she had to live on."' **Luke 21:1-4**

Time for a bit of controversy here. In far too many churches, I hear teaching on tithing that doesn't mention the New Testament's principles, and these verses in particular. Let's be honest, giving a tenth is good news for the rich but bad news for the poor. If you earn a million quid a year after tax, chances are that you can struggle on with the £900K that's left over after your tithe; but what if you earn only 10 grand a year? The £1,000 you give as your tithe is going to really hurt.

So, two comments today. First, to the richer among us: I want to challenge you to think about your giving. Is it actually sacrificial? Are you truly giving in a way you think God is pleased with? Don't just take refuge in the 10% principle and think you are doing enough. That is following the law and not your heart. Which is the more New Testament approach?

Second, if you don't have much in the way of money or material possessions, never forget the power of the widow's offering. You can be sure that God sees your heart and understands the sacrifice involved in giving even a few quid away. Personally, I believe He sees our giving very differently from us. As these verses tell us, a few coins from someone who has very little is worth far more to Him than we may think.

Prayer: Please give me a generous heart and inspire me to give sacrificially. Amen.

28/Back at ya!

'Do not judge, and you will not be judged. Do not condemn, and you will not be condemned. Forgive, and you will be forgiven. Give, and it will be given to you. A good measure, pressed down, shaken together and running over, will be poured into your lap. For with the measure you use, it will be measured to you.' **Luke 6:37-38**

Interesting, this one. It's often said that if you go through life with a smile, people will smile back at you. You often find, too, that the most generous people are more often on the receiving end of generosity. Again, people who give others the benefit of the doubt and believe the best and don't judge tend to be more at peace, experience less disappointment and have more friends!

Much of this is simply the basis, humanly speaking, of living life well. However, it seems to me from these verses that when we live in the way Jesus asks us to, something supernatural happens as well. When we live generous, grace-filled, outward-facing lives, it seems that God pours His blessing onto them as well. I'm not pushing some half-baked, unthought-through prosperity teaching here, I'm talking about God rewarding you for pouring your life out.

It's worth bearing this in mind when the temptation surfaces to be mean with your time or money, or ungracious about a colleague or a member of your family or whatever. Believe the best of those around you, choose to see past the problems to the potential and God will treat you the same way. Keep that in mind the next time you are in a meeting at work and the politics kicks off. Keep it in mind when the offering plate comes round at church. And have it in the forefront of your mind when you are dealing with someone who is really hacking you off!

Prayer: Father, inspire in me a generous and grace-filled approach to people and possessions. Amen.

29/Lonesome

'Very early in the morning, while it was still dark, Jesus got up, left the house and went off to a solitary place, where he prayed.' **Mark 1:35**

I was talking to a mate recently when he said to me: 'Sometimes I just sit down on the sofa and do nothing but think.' Now, that may seem like a rather mundane thing to say, until you sit quietly on a sofa yourself and ponder it. How often do you take time out to do nothing but process your thoughts and think things through properly? Probably not very often. Normally there is background noise and all sorts of distractions and communications vying for your attention.

A few years ago, all we had were letters and payphones. When I was at uni in 1990, we didn't have texts or emails, Facebook, Twitter and so on. Amazing, when you think about it! In these verses, Jesus models a form of prayer that we are losing touch with today. Traditionally, we called it a 'quiet time' (though personally I don't like that term, as it sounds a bit weird to most people who aren't Christians, and very twee). Whatever you want to call it, though, it involves being in a place where there are no distractions. For Jesus, that was early in the morning when it was still dark and no one could see Him. I don't think that means that for us it *has* to be early – I just believe that we need to find a solitary place, free from interruption, to think and, crucially, pray. Most men struggle with not doing stuff, but I see this as an essential daily discipline.

And one final word: if we must have a label for this kind of time out, let's not call it a 'retreat'! The British Army never retreats, it makes a tactical withdrawal ...

Prayer: Father, meet with me in quiet places where there are no distractions. Prompt me to take time out to think things through and pray. Speak to me then through Your Holy Spirit and strengthen my walk with You. Amen.

30/Force 110

'That day when evening came, he said to his disciples, "Let us go over to the other side." Leaving the crowd behind, they took him along, just as he was, in the boat ... A furious squall came up, and the waves broke over the boat, so that it was nearly swamped. Jesus was in the stern, sleeping on a cushion. The disciples woke him and said to him, "Teacher, don't you care if we drown?" He got up, rebuked the wind and said to the waves, "Quiet! Be still!" Then the wind died down and it was completely calm. He said to his disciples, "Why are you so afraid? Do you still have no faith?"'

Mark 4:35-40

It's good, as men, to be reminded that we don't have what it takes to calm a raging storm. It's even better to be reminded that we follow a Man who does! Storms are an inevitable part of life, and sometimes the gale can strike when you least expect it. A sudden redundancy, a spat of serious ill health, an unaffordable bill, you know the kind of thing – stuff that makes us afraid because it's beyond our control.

I remember doing an emergency hospital visit to a family whose son had just been involved in a very bad accident. When I turned up, the news was grim and the medics were telling his parents to prepare for the worst. What happened next floored me. His parents held hands and knelt in the public waiting-room and, basically, said: 'Father, this is out of our control. We hand our son back to You.' It was incredibly moving.

As it turned out, their son, by the grace of God, pulled through. But whatever storms come your way, keep your head and remember you follow a Man who has authority over even the elements.

Prayer: Father, I place my trust in You, who made the universe and gave Your Son authority over it. I know I can't fix everything. Help me to rely on You more. Amen.

31/Denial

'Then he called the crowd to him along with his disciples and said: "Whoever wants to be my disciple must deny themselves and take up their cross and follow me. For whoever wants to save their life will lose it, but whoever loses their life for me and for the gospel will save it."' **Mark 8:34-35**

Deny yourself? That's a bit radical for our day and age, innit? We're in the 'please yourself' era, if we're honest about it. There's no point in kidding ourselves here: most of us don't lead lives of self-denial as a conscious, ongoing daily expression of following Jesus. So, what do these verses really mean? It's fascinating, because at this point Jesus is suggesting to everyone listening what His fate will be – crucifixion – and is basically saying that anyone who really wants to be His follower must be prepared to go down the same route!

That's why I don't think that, in reality, this is just about giving up your gym membership or whatever. It goes deeper than that. Let's put it this way: When push comes to shove, are we prepared to give up *whatever* God asks of us? Would we, if it was ever to come to this, be ready to lay down our lives for the gospel cause? You might well think that question a bit OTT – it's not very likely in our culture, is it? – but the horrific truth is that, outside the strange bubble we live in in the UK, on average someone is martyred for their Christian faith every five minutes! In the time it has taken you to read this, somewhere in the world a brother or sister may have lost their life for following Jesus.

So, today we should not only ask ourselves how serious we really are about our faith, but we should also pause to remember those who are suffering pressure and persecution because they refuse to deny Jesus.

Prayer: Today, why not sit for a while in silent thought?

32/ The greatest commandment

'One of the teachers of the law came and heard them debating. Noticing that Jesus had given them a good answer, he asked him, "Of all the commandments, which is the most important?" "The most important one," answered Jesus, "is this: 'Hear, O Israel: the Lord our God, the Lord is one. Love the Lord your God with all your heart and with all your soul and with all your mind and with all your strength.'"' **Mark 12:28-30**

It's called the *Shema* and it derives from Deuteronomy 6:4. Jesus is here going back to His roots and affirming a profound and solid tradition. Every day, without fail, devout Jews say this, and it is what has brought them through centuries of persecution: from the hard times in the desert to the medieval massacres, to the concentration camps. It is a declaration that has gone deep into their psyche. It's why in the Warsaw Ghetto in the Second World War they set up schools and even an orchestra, even though doing such things could get you hanged by the Nazis. Women had babies, even though giving birth meant the death penalty!

I think this understanding should mean a lot to us. If we don't just pay lip service to God but truly love Him with all our will and all our strength, then that has to inform the way we face up to life in all its challenges. It'll inform the way we deal with work, family and other people. Our devotion to Him will mean that we won't want to hurt Him by our attitudes or actions. It'll mean we won't want to waste any opportunity to tell people about Him. Crucially, it'll mean (as it did for the Jews under persecution) that we live with a sense of hope, because that is what loving God gives us.

Perhaps the *Shema* should become a prayer of ours?

Prayer: Hear, O Israel: the Lord our God, the Lord is one. I will love the Lord my God with all my heart and with all my soul, and with all my mind and with all my strength. Amen.

33/True grit

'Going a little farther, he fell to the ground and prayed that if possible the hour might pass from him. "*Abba*, Father," he said, "everything is possible for you. Take this cup from me. Yet not what I will, but what you will."' **Mark 14:35-36**

At this point in Mark, the end game is in plain sight. We can't even begin to conceive what it must have been like for Jesus. He now knew not only the horror of the manner of execution He was soon to suffer, but also that as He died He would be bearing the full, crushing weight of the world's sin. What I find totally stunning here, however, is the fact that Jesus clearly had a choice about whether He went through with it or not. At this moment, the whole destiny of the human race was hanging on His decision to submit *His* will to that of His Father. You get the sense that on the one hand He was pleading with God to spare Him but on the other hand He was desperate to do His will.

There's something very human about this. I may not face crucifixion but I can relate to the feeling of struggling to do what is right. In the verses leading up to this passage we see Jesus under pressure, getting seriously stressed – well, that's an understatement! – or, as the NIV puts it, 'deeply troubled'. This tells us that it's OK when we feel like that ourselves. It's OK when we struggle to do stuff that we know we ought to do as Christians. It's OK to tell God honestly that it's all getting too much.

The bottom line, though, is that when the time came for the rubber to hit the road, Jesus was obedient to God. So, yes, we can wrestle and struggle, but let's be men who do what's required when we need to step up to the plate.

Prayer: Strengthen me, Father, to be a man who does Your will and not my own. Help me to follow the example of Jesus, who overcame His fear to be obedient to You. Amen.

34/Flesh v. spirit

'Then he returned to his disciples and found them sleeping. "Simon," he said to Peter, "are you asleep? Couldn't you keep watch for one hour? Watch and pray so that you will not fall into temptation. The spirit is willing, but the flesh is weak."' **Mark 14:37-38**

I totally get this. I'm a pretty full-on bloke when it comes to my faith – in fact, I don't really do anything by halves. When I took up cycling, I ended up pedalling from Land's End to John o'Groats, then from Calais to Nice (over the Alps!) and from Nice to Naples. Each trip took nine days. When I started jogging, I ended up running a marathon. When I became a follower of Jesus, I wound up becoming a church leader and evangelist. I can't quite help myself!

And therein lies the problem: I can't quite help myself. If I'm brutally frank about it, despite my tendency to go all-in with whatever I'm doing, there is always the possibility that I could cave in at any time. That's what happened to Peter. He was the full-on guy. He is the man in Luke's account who was first on the scene at the resurrection. He's the guy who drew his sword and took a man's ear off when they came to arrest Jesus. He was a working man and a man's man. And yet, when it came to the crunch, he couldn't face up and he denied Jesus. I think that's potentially me. You don't know what you'd do until you're in those sort of situations, but I recognise that, even as a full-on bloke, I have my weaknesses. Jesus knew that Peter was the same and that's why He told him to pray that he would stay strong.

So, make it a regular habit, no matter how well you think you have it together, to pray for strength, so that when the tests come you won't fall at the first hurdle.

Prayer: Strengthen my character and resolve so that, despite my passion for You and Your kingdom, I won't fall when the pressure is on and temptations crowd in around me. Amen.

[PSALM SURFING]

35/Trust

'In you, LORD my God, I put my trust.' **Psalm 25:1**

There are lots of things, as guys, we can put our trust in. We are shocking for thinking, even if only subconsciously, that we can get most things sorted ourselves. We're not good at the 'being dependent' thing. The fact is, though, that in reality we put our trust in all kinds of things other than God.

About a week ago as I write this, a couple in their early forties won 148 million quid on the lottery, putting them in at number 516 in Britain's Rich List. Now, I don't know about you but even though I don't actually take part in the lottery, I still find it easy to imagine how I would spend the money if it were me! And just for a fleeting moment it crossed my mind that I should go out and get a ticket. Stupid, really. It's just something else that people are pinning their hopes on other than God.

When you do a sharp and clear analysis of your life, you begin to realise that, in fact, there are loads of different areas where we place our trust. We have all sorts of insurance, health cover and investment schemes. In fact, when you take out insurance for your house, there are so many options you can tick it almost feels like you're insuring your insurance! Now, some of this is sensible, of course, and some of it is required by law. There has to be a balance, though. I think it's a good question for a man who follows Jesus to ask himself every so often: How much do I really trust God to provide and care for me and my loved ones? Am I really living as if He is the ultimate source of everything I have, or do I think it's actually down to me?

Go on, have a ponder. Can you say Psalm 25:1 and truly mean it?

Prayer: God, I place my trust and my hope solidly in You today. Amen.

36/Shame?

'I trust in you; do not let me be
put to shame, nor let my enemies
triumph over me.' **Psalm 25:2**

Most of us don't have enemies in the way David
did as a man who was often at war, or battling
politically. Some of us may be in the armed forces,
though, and may have to face an adversary who
is out to kill and destroy. More on that sort of
threat another time, because this verse is about
people who were out to stab David in the back
by trying to shame him or stitch him up. We
know this because the psalm goes on to talk
about treachery. So, what do you do when you're
surrounded by people who are out to get you?
I was stitched up badly one time when I was
in banking. It's a bit too complicated to go into
here, but suffice to say I ended up taking a hit
and losing a possible promotion because of the
deviousness of a manager I hadn't seen coming.
What do you do in a situation like that? From my
perspective, all I could do was tell God that I knew

I hadn't done anything wrong and resolve not to play the same game and look for revenge.

In that particular case – and I know it doesn't always work out like this – the manager concerned was made redundant a few months later and I was promoted within half a year. I learned that sometimes you just have to keep your head and your integrity and trust that God will deal with things. As it turned out, I was vindicated and God didn't allow me to be put to shame. Partly, I think, because I didn't play the same games as my 'enemy' did.

Prayer: Keep in me a heart that puts its trust in You, God and stop me in my tracks if ever I start to respond to politics in an unhealthy way. Don't let me be put to shame when the tough times come and help me not to surrender my integrity. Amen.

37/You want me to do what?!

'Show me your ways, LORD, teach me your paths. Guide me in your truth and teach me, for you are God my Saviour, and my hope is in you all day long. Remember, LORD, your great mercy and love, for they are from of old.' **Psalm 25:4-6**

Following Jesus is pretty countercultural, so it's a bold prayer when we say: 'Show me Your ways, Lord.' You can be pretty sure that your way of dealing with things and His way are going to be poles apart. The world loves revenge but Jesus says to forgive. We want stuff but Jesus tells us to be generous and to give. The world loves to moan but the Bible tells us always to be thankful. I could go on.

How about the classic scenario where your neighbour's fence blows down but he insists that it's your fence, even though the title deeds and plan you've carefully kept copies of show that it's not your problem. What do you do? Go to war and fall out for years or just swallow your pride and fix the fence? I'm not telling you what you should do here, I'm just raising the question that has now become as Christian as quiche: What would Jesus do? The reason that question is so powerful is because, most times, what *He* would do is not what we would.

So, those of us who want to become more like Jesus need to give Him full permission to do some attitude and character surgery. In my experience, once we pray this prayer He starts to take us into situations that press our buttons. After all, how can He train us if He doesn't chuck us into the very scenarios that tend to get to the heart of who we are ...?

Prayer: Show me Your ways, Lord; teach me Your paths. Guide me in Your truth and teach me, for You are God my Saviour. Amen.

38/What muck-up?

'Do not remember the sins of my youth and my rebellious ways; according to your love remember me, for you, LORD, are good.' **Psalm 25:7**

We all stuff up at some point. Some of us probably feel like we stuff up every week. The problem for most of us is that we live with a sense of guilt or disappointment because of mistakes we have made in the past. Regret can be such a toxic emotion! Couple it with guilt and you're on a hiding to nothing.

Well, here's the deal: God always finishes what He starts. So many men live with a feeling that actually He has put them on a shelf and forgotten them. So many have a vision or a sense of call to do something for Him that, for whatever reason, has never quite happened. Many guys I talk to live perpetually with a feeling of 'I nearly made it for God but not quite', sort of thing – either because they feel they failed really to step out in faith when the crunch came or because some sort of sin was going on that they never quite conquered. Even the mighty King David (who was, as you know, more than capable himself of stuffing up!) had this feeling.

So, like David, sometimes we simply need to repent, get on our knees and ask God to forgive us. Then we need to get up, brush off the dust and the dirt and crack on, trusting 'that he who began a good work in you will carry it on to completion until the day of Christ Jesus' (Phil. 1:6).

Prayer: My heart is for You, God, so forgive me for holding back because of past stuff in my life. Thank You that You are a God of many chances. Thank You for Your grace and forgiveness. Amen.

39/Know-all

> 'He guides the humble in what is right and teaches them his way.'
> **Psalm 25:9**

No one likes a know-all. Remember the Harry Enfield sketches? He had the bloke in the pub who used to go off on a rant that would end: 'I'd say, "Damon Hill, NO!!"' And then there was the other guy, a complete idiot, whose catchphrase was 'You don't want to do it like that, you want to do it like *this*.' They were totally exaggerated caricatures, but they were based on truth and a real laugh.

The fact is, of course, that many of us men have a tendency to be a bit like both of those characters. It's amazing how quickly you can become an expert! When I was watching the Olympics, I started to score the diving and use the commentators' lingo as if I actually knew what I was on about. I did the same with the running, the long jump and even the eventing. You get the drift. All blokes tend to be experts on everything (especially after a pint of ale – and sometimes less)!

It gets a bit more toxic when we become unteachable, though. I think this is at the heart of what it means to be humble. The humble man never stops being teachable and never stops learning. You want to be more like Jesus? Then keep yourself open to hearing His voice. It may mean having to listen to some painful truths, of course. It may also mean that you have to be prepared to learn from people you think are not as well-informed as you. I remember as a new church leader, fresh out of Bible college, being told that if I couldn't take a lesson on a finer point of theology from an old dear called Ethel, I was probably in the wrong job ...

Prayer: Build a humble heart in me and keep me attentive to Your voice. Amen.

40/ Where is your strength from?

'My eyes are ever on the LORD, for only he will release my feet from the snare.' Psalm 25:15

One of my mates had an epiphany a while back. He had gone climbing with another mate, only to see him fall past him head-first, accompanied by the lump of rock he had anchored himself to moments before because he thought it was totally secure.

You'll be pleased to know that they both survived (although the other guy had multiple fractures) after they were choppered off the mountain. My mate's epiphany was this: it struck him that when the chips are seriously down, there is only one direction you can look, really, and that is up. We're sort of touching on the self-sufficiency theme again here, but it's a crucial truth for us to get to grips with. My mate realised that, humanly speaking, it was potentially game-over. He's a bright guy, fit and motivated and mostly able to sort things out. It took this experience for him to grasp the fact that, ultimately, his life was fragile and he was highly vulnerable. He could have died.

The heart of this verse, for me, is David basically saying to God: 'Look, I know I'm a capable guy – I'm pretty good with a sword and all that – but I need Your help and strength or I'm done for.' I think that's a really good place to be. I don't know what you're facing today or what stuff is crowding in around you, but wherever you are, whatever is kicking off, just keep looking up and place your trust in God!

Prayer: I place my trust and hope in You, God. I look to You for help and strength and I do not, and will not, depend on my own capabilities. Amen.

41/How to be a winner

'... we'd better get on with it. Strip down, start running – and never quit!' **Hebrews 12:1 (The Message)**

I like running. I developed this strange passion before I became a Christian, while serving in the Royal Navy – mainly because I was bored and needed something to do apart from drink alcohol and watch porn (which seemed to be the main alternatives back then). The Bible talks a lot about running races. Sometimes our 'walk with God' can seem like a sprint, sometimes the hurdles – or else the marathon with a few steeplechase barriers thrown in for good measure!

Wherever you are in that race today, you can improve your performance by getting help and guidance from others. In a marathon, an athlete takes on fuel and water as they run and you can have your coach cycling alongside you offering advice on tactics and so on. It's really helpful, too, to have some good partners who will run with you, no matter how long or steep the road is. Likewise, in running the race of life we need to listen to God's Spirit, who is the ultimate Coach, and we also need good mates around us, who will support us and sustain us whatever happens. We need to be careful about what we consume – for example, do the things that we look at, the places we go and the way we spend our time help our relationship with God or draw us away from Him? And we have to know when to ease up (particularly with regard to 'church' stuff, maybe) so that we don't get burnt out and have to quit.

Prayer: Father, show me what I need to do to ensure that I will finish the race. Amen.

True friends stab you in the front!
OSCAR WILDE

42/The everyday plod

'So let's keep focused on that goal, those of us who want everything God has for us. If any of you have something else in mind, something less than total commitment, God will clear your blurred vision – you'll see it yet! Now that we're on the right track, let's stay on it.'
Philippians 3:15-16 (The Message)

Routine training (or practice for anything, be it sport, music or exams) can be a real challenge. Training runs on board ship when we were at sea were hard work. Twelve laps of the ship to the mile, turning corner after corner, with the same old view: grey paint and the sea! Nothing to break it up, you just kept plodding round – it was that or nothing. I had doors opened in my face, and on one occasion, when I wasn't concentrating, I slipped and almost ended up over the side. Sometimes I really didn't feel like going up on deck at all – let's just have another cuppa and watch a movie, wait till we get back to port and I can run in a straight line with some more interesting scenery!

Do you ever feel like you are just plodding along with God? Same old same old every day – even getting distracted and nearly going over the side? But, of course, if we want to be ready on 'race day' we need to keep training or else we will lose our edge. We need to keep our muscles in trim, keep our heart rates going – and we can only do that by keeping up with the boring runs. Much of the time, our relationship with God is one of routine, with prayers seeming not to be answered, stuff that distracts us and constant temptations to quit. But it's here that we just have to grit our teeth and get on with it, trusting that the everyday plod will pay dividends in due course.

Prayer: Help me to keep focused when life seems to be a boring plod. I don't want to lose concentration and end up 'over the side'! Amen.

43/Check the map!

'But you need to stick it out, staying with God's plan so you'll be there for the promised completion.'

Hebrews 10:36 (The Message)

Arriving in foreign ports was great for us runners. We could explore – just go off and run. After days of plodding round the ship, it was time to take a bit of a risk and go for it. God wants us to do that as well: to take a risk sometimes, have just a vague plan or target and then go for it. We are blokes, after all!

Once, when my ship put in at Naples, three of us wanted to run up Vesuvius. We looked at the map, checked how to get there from the docks and were ready to go. But then someone who had been in Naples before said he could drop us off at the foot of the mountain. Great! When we got there, we started to run up this road – which soon became a track and then petered out completely. We must have missed a turning! We started back down, thoroughly disheartened, and when we met a local we asked him the way to the top of Vesuvius. 'Vesuvius?' he said, looking towards a completely different mountain in the middle distance ...

God doesn't always give us a definite route, it's often just a destination – but then others seem to have a better idea than us and we listen to them and, without us realising it, we head off in the wrong direction and end up running up the wrong mountain. So, listen to God, make your plans but keep checking that you are on the right track!

Prayer: Thank You that You guide and direct us. Help me always to listen to Your voice and not get diverted by other people's 'good ideas'! Amen.

44/Keep on to the end!

'Don't compare yourself with others. Each of you must take responsibility for doing the creative best you can with your own life.'
Galatians 6:5 (The Message)

The Rock of Gibraltar offers a 900-foot climb in 2.6 miles, and visiting ships always stage a race there. So far on this ship I had run that race twice and won one, lost one – just beating my running partner on one occasion and just losing to him on the other. The next time we stopped off there, our crewmates were betting on which of us would win this time, so we made a secret pact that we would cross the line together and share the spoils! However, as we approached the finish, neck-and-neck as we had agreed, a young lad who didn't know the script tore past us and won. Well, it's not the winning that's important, is it, it's the taking part – though my mate still nearly threw that lad off the rock!

Humanly speaking, of course we want to win the race; but in the race of life we must not worry about where the rest of the field is. It isn't a competition, it's a team effort, with mates who run with you in good times and bad. Don't waste time comparing yourself with others – we are in this race to finish and we are aiming for our mates to finish, too. Other people may well seem to be doing better or going faster, but God wants us to finish with Him! All that training, listening to the Coach, learning the rules and getting His guidance, plodding along, nearly going over the side, getting lost, turning back when you've gone off-track – the whole point is to cross the finish line, and to get as many others over it as possible. That's how you win the prize!

Prayer: Help me not to compare where I and my mates have got to in life, but simply to focus on getting over the line and bringing others with me. Amen.

45/ Boldness be my friend

'Then Peter said, "Silver or gold I do not have, but what I do have I give you. In the name of Jesus Christ of Nazareth, walk." Taking him by the right hand, he helped him up, and instantly the man's feet and ankles became strong. He jumped to his feet and began to walk. Then he went with them into the temple courts, walking and jumping, and praising God.' **Acts 3:6-8**

Regardless of the miracle – which is sensational – what I really love about this story is the sheer boldness of Peter. He just seems to be in the zone here, and acting with a spiritual authority that is totally off the chart! Having witnessed the resurrection, he had utter confidence in Christ and had no doubt at all that He was coming back. And he thought this would be soon – which, of course, must have given him an added edge.

I aspire to have that same boldness and I try my best. Not so long ago, I was walking past the Norwegian embassy in London when I saw an Asian woman sitting on the steps, smoking and crying. I had that prompt that you sometimes get, so I took a deep breath and asked if she was OK. Her reply was astonishing: 'God has forgotten me since the day I was born!' To cut a long story short, she was a Norwegian national, stranded in London and with no money to get home. We sat together and prayed, and within a few minutes someone pitched up from the embassy and told me they would take her in and sort it all out.

I love that. A moment of supernatural intervention on the streets of London. May boldness be my friend!

Prayer: May I have the courage to be a witness and an ambassador, wherever You send me, wherever I may find myself. Amen.

46/Fair shares

'All the believers were one in heart and mind. No one claimed that any of their possessions was their own, but they shared everything they had. With great power the apostles continued to testify to the resurrection of the Lord Jesus. And God's grace was so powerfully at work in them all that there was no needy person among them. For from time to time those who owned land or houses sold them, brought the money from the sales and put it at the apostles' feet, and it was distributed to anyone who had need.' **Acts 4:32-35**

You could say that what we're reading about here is the birth of communism – but that would be a mistake. In the Old Testament, there was a radical principle called 'jubilee', which involved the cancelling of debts, the return of inherited land that had been sold to pay bills and the liberation of those who had actually had to sell themselves into bonded labour. It was intended by God to ensure a fair society where the gulf between rich and poor could never become too wide. The Israelites never practised it, however, probably because it was just too tough!

Now, though, post Pentecost, the spirit of jubilee was written into believers' hearts and it meant some revolutionary stuff. It seems that sharing possessions was the norm. We know from Acts 2 they 'had everything in common' and as a result no one went without. 'Jubilee' had become a constant way of life among these early Christians.

This is hugely challenging for us today. When was the last time we practised such extreme generosity? Are there people around us who obviously need help but are being ignored? I think it would be massively powerful to see an army of men rising up who lived radically generous lives.

Prayer: Create in me a radically generous heart. Show me who I can give practical or financial help to and grant me the will to do it. Amen.

47/Clash of the kingdoms

'Those who had been scattered preached the word wherever they went. Philip went down to a city in Samaria and proclaimed the Messiah there. When the crowds heard Philip and saw the signs he performed, they all paid close attention to what he said. For with shrieks, impure spirits came out of many, and many who were paralysed or lame were healed. So there was great joy in that city.'
Acts 8:4-8

I guess you would pay close attention to a speaker if impure spirits started coming out of people screaming. It would kind of validate what he was saying, wouldn't it? What I love about this story is the sense of two kingdoms clashing. Satanic forces were being harassed and disturbed because Jesus was being proclaimed with authority and power. Of course, it wasn't all plain sailing for the apostles. Remember that nine out of twelve of them were martyred! However, despite all of this, it seems abundantly clear that the presence of a man of God has a profound impact spiritually, wherever he is. You may not see impure spirits coming out of people but rest assured that the enemy knows about you and considers you (assuming you are walking with Jesus) to be dangerous.

I think we forget about this side of our faith walk. We are, in effect, men in conflict with the forces of darkness. Try to keep that in mind, at work and at home. Sometimes the difficulties we face are just life and stuff, but sometimes they can most certainly be a result of demonic activity. We don't talk about this enough, or pray about it. I don't mean we should see a demon behind every filing cabinet but I do think we should not be surprised when we meet opposition or see strange reactions to stuff we are trying to do – especially if there is a kingdom agenda behind it.

Prayer: Keep my eyes open to the reality of the spiritual battle that is raging around me. Amen.

48/Hold the line

'Even from your own number men will arise and distort the truth in order to draw away disciples after them. So be on your guard! Remember that for three years I never stopped warning each of you night and day with tears.' **Acts 20:30-31**

Paul could see it coming. He had relentlessly preached the good news without compromise and had done his best to make sure that it sank in. Then, before he got out of Dodge to head for Rome, he issued this warning that some men would make subtle changes to the truth in order to get a following for themselves. Same old same old, I guess.

I'm always a bit wary when someone comes up with some brand-new insight from Scripture that apparently had always been hidden before! I keep saying to the guys at CVM, the ministry I lead: 'We're about simple and plain, straight-down-the-line gospel truth – nothing new!' In our opinion, the gospel is spectacular enough and we've got enough to do trying to tell men all over the UK about it.

So, let's hold the line, guard against the rubbish and be totally committed to making Jesus known – rather than getting our itching ears tickled by the latest prayer strategy to get a new Mercedes! (I've got to be honest with you: I tune into some so-called Christian channel to see some guy telling me to send money so that I can have a prosperity handkerchief or a bottle of miracle water, and everything in me wants to put him up against a wall and politely ask him to stop. Basically, in my opinion that kind of stuff stinks and it's theft.) Let's keep it real and keep it straight down the line.

Prayer: Thank You, Father, for the gospel. Thank You for Jesus. Help me to make the gospel the cause of my life and the driving force of my relationship with You. Amen.

[NO MESSING]

49/Qualifications

'An elder must be blameless, faithful to his wife, a man whose children believe and are not open to the charge of being wild and disobedient. Since an overseer manages God's household, he must be blameless – not overbearing, not quick-tempered, not given to drunkenness, not violent, not pursuing dishonest gain.' **Titus 1:6-7**

As far as I can, I like to take the Bible at face value. The challenges it presents become even starker when you don't try to fudge them. Here is a list of qualifications a man must have in order to become a leader or elder. I remember hearing a well-known preacher once saying that you need to take some statements in the Bible lightly. He cited this passage as an example and said: 'You would laugh if I told you that we actually used these verses as a list of qualifications for eldership!' I wasn't laughing, because the previous week we had laid hands on some new elders in our church and we had chosen them on the basis of whether they matched up to this list.

So, I would say this: who you are as a person profoundly affects the culture and character of those you lead. If you aspire to leadership, this is your measure. Even if you don't, you should certainly aim for these standards. They make sense, too. For example, if you lose your rag easily, the people who work for you or live with you will take their cue from you and you'll end up with an angry department or an angry home. It's interesting, too, to ponder the idea that an elder should have children who believe and aren't wild and disobedient. So, aim high and take these verses as a standard for your work and family life.

One final thing: I know a lot of blokes enjoy a beer or a glass of red but let's make sure we keep our necks firmly wound in and don't overdo it. More on this later!

Prayer: Strengthen my resolve to be an ever more godly man. Show me where I need to change my ways significantly. Amen.

50/The beer's on you!

'Rather, he must be hospitable, one who loves what is good, who is self-controlled, upright, holy and disciplined.' **Titus 1:8**

Let's arrow in on the hospitality thing. I felt really challenged about this some years ago when I was a senior pastor and we were taking on a new year-out volunteer for our youth work. We were a large church with several congregations and I didn't really think it was a good idea to have the young woman I was going to be boss of living in my house. Besides that, my wife and I were in a small, three-bedroom semi – well, more like 2.5 bedrooms, actually – and we had two small kids.

However, when I let it be known that we needed someone to host this volunteer for a few months, no one came forward. Eventually, I realised that God was speaking to me and so she came and lived with us. We cleared out the second-biggest bedroom, got the kids bunk beds and put them in the box room, and opened our home. I learned a lot about myself that year! We had our family life opened up for someone else to see at close range and I learned that I was a bit precious over some routines and possessions in a way that was completely stupid. I learned that what I said from the front of church really needed to be demonstrated at home as well. It was a challenging time but in the end it was really fulfilling.

I once asked a guy much older than me what he had learned about Jesus in his long walk with Him. His immediate response was: 'He wants us to spend more time with people.' That's a challenge for us blokes, but let's work out how we can rise to it.

Prayer: Give me a generous and hospitable heart. Help me to open up my life more and share the good things You have given me. Amen.

51/Fnarr fnarr

'To the pure, all things are pure, but to those who are corrupted and do not believe, nothing is pure.' **Titus 1:15**

We Brits are the masters of innuendo. We're the island people who gave the world the smutty seaside postcard, 'Carry On' films and Benny Hill. It's quite an impressive record, really, for such a small country! The problems arise when we start to see double meanings everywhere and sexualise every comment and interaction. For men of God, that's a step too far. You know what it's like: you're in a work meeting or in the changing room at the gym and someone makes a remark and everyone starts to crack up. Now, sometimes it's healthy to laugh, of course, especially if it's a blatantly obvious faux pas; but it gets pretty toxic when everything is about sex and, quite frankly, smut.

The problem is that we get numbed to it when it's so constant. There's obviously a balance to be struck here. We don't want to become puritanical, nightmare believers who go around smashing stuff up like Oliver Cromwell's men or acting totally miserable and grieved with the world. But let's be clear about this: you can lead a pure life without being a killjoy. I remember the first time I ever went to church, it was full of really godly people but they all looked totally fed up. I couldn't work out why they wanted to be there, to be honest. So, let's not go down that route. On the other hand, we do need to keep our hearts pure.

So, draw a line in the sand, once you've decided where it should be, and resolve that you're not going to cross it.

Prayer: Help me to decide where to draw the line and help me to stand firm and keep my heart pure. Amen.

52/Matching up

'They claim to know God, but by their actions they deny him. They are detestable, disobedient and unfit for doing anything good.'

Titus 1:16

There were occasions during the apartheid era in South Africa – I was told of one once by a pastor who actually witnessed it – when Christians who had sung their hearts out in a church meeting, prayed in tongues and shared prophetic words, later took part in the murder of people from the black population. I know that's a really extreme and totally disgusting example of the way our actions sometimes don't measure up to our words, but on a smaller scale I see this kind of discrepancy all around me. The bloke who says he is a follower of Jesus but hangs on to bitterness and refuses to forgive other people. Or the believer who is hugely ungenerous, or who has the foulest language or temper. How about the hotel that reported an increase in the use of its in-room porn channel when there was a

Christian conference on? What on earth is going on there?

As I write this, I've just had yet another report sent to me of a pastor with a significant ministry who has just left his wife and kids to go off with a much younger woman. It makes me feel sick, partly because another soldier has fallen, partly because of what it means for his abandoned family – and partly because I know that deep down I, too, am capable of blowing up. There but for the grace of God ...

We're in a fight and we need to take care to be consistent in what we say we are and the way we actually live our lives. Anything less than that and we fall under the condemnation of Titus 1:16.

Prayer: May my actions match my words and may my character and my conduct always speak of You. Amen.

53/ Be like a slave

'Teach slaves to be subject to their masters in everything, to try to please them, not to talk back to them, and not to steal from them, but to show that they can be fully trusted, so that in every way they will make the teaching about God our Saviour attractive.' **Titus 2:9-10**

We are not slaves. If we're not self-employed, we have employment rights and unions and sick leave and we can take our employers to a tribunal if we think we've been unfairly treated. Despite this, however, there's some great stuff in these verses for all of us fellas who have a boss. The temptations are so strong to moan and whine about those in authority. Sometimes, we start to play little games to vent our frustrations. I was talking to a bloke in a church recently and he made this throwaway comment: 'I'm starting to have fun with my new boss. She's not that savvy, so I'm making her think I really appreciate her –

but I'll probably end up with her job!' What kind of mindset is that for someone who knows Jesus?

Our attitude should be to want to give our very best to both our employer and our immediate manager and to keep our actions free from politicking, manipulation and game-playing. Ultimately, the aim is to make the gospel more attractive, so let's watch ourselves keenly and always act for the benefit and not the detriment of those above us. Even if they wind us up!

Prayer: Make me an encouragement and a blessing to those in authority over me. Help me to encourage my bosses and not play games that bring them down or make their lives difficult. Amen.

54/ Exit door

'For the grace of God has appeared that offers salvation to all people. It teaches us to say "No" to ungodliness and worldly passions, and to live self-controlled, upright and godly lives in this present age.'
Titus 2:11-12

When we first received Jesus into our lives, chances are we were pretty bowled over by it all. I can remember for nearly a month feeling like I was literally on cloud nine. The world seemed to be a different place. To my astonishment, certain things I had been doing stopped having any attraction for me. My language cleaned up pretty much overnight and, while I still loved going out with my mates, I no longer wanted to drink myself under the table with them. It was almost a total character transplant. Not sinning seemed, to be honest, pretty easy – for the first month or two.

Then, slowly but surely, the battle started to get tougher and previous sins began to make a comeback for some reason. Nightmare! Now, I would love to say that standing firm has been easy, but (being totally realistic about it all) I have to admit that it hasn't been. Yes, God's grace is present, but what we need to realise is this: we have to decide to stand firm, in response to what God has shown us and taught us. He won't stand firm for us or take the temptations away. What happens is this: as *we* start to exercise self-control, fight back and get the mastery over our lack of discipline, the temptations diminish. In short, we have to man up and say 'No' and then take the exit door that is always provided for us. So, next time you feel tempted, say 'No!' and get out of there!

Prayer: Show me the exit door that You always provide and give me the determination and strength to use it whenever I am tempted. Amen.

55/Slander

'Remind the people to be subject to rulers and authorities, to be obedient, to be ready to do whatever is good, to slander no one, to be peaceable and considerate, and always to be gentle towards everyone.' **Titus 3:1-2**

OK, so we pretty much know that, as followers of Jesus, the authorities should have nothing to fear from us. We should be the most law-abiding of citizens and the most up-to-date with our taxes. We know that we should be known as those who do good and not ill, as men of peace who are considerate and gentle. It's tough at times – I find it tough always to be gentle, for instance – but we totally get that we should be like this.

The word that really jumps out at me, however, is 'slander'. I find it really interesting that it comes right in the middle of a load of stuff about the way we treat people. Sitting here thinking about it, I can see why it's so important. When someone sidles up to me and starts moaning about someone behind their back, I can't help but wonder if they're doing the same thing about me to someone else. So, when I'm in a meeting or out for dinner and people start talking about someone else in a slightly malicious way, I just clam up. I can feel the temptation to join in sometimes, but I just don't like what I can feel it doing to my heart. I'm also fully aware that you tend to reap what you sow!

Prayer: When people around me are putting the knife in, remind me to button it and stay out of the conversation. May I be known as a man who has only good things to say about others. Amen.

56/ Large doner, please

'Do not join those who drink too much wine or gorge themselves on meat, for drunkards and gluttons become poor, and drowsiness clothes them in rags.' **Proverbs 23:20-21**

Now, I know it's not everyone's thing but every so often I do get a bit of an urge for a kebab. That's probably not a good thing, to be honest. Check this out: a kebab contains more than twice the recommended daily intake of salt and the fat content is so high it's equivalent to about a wine-glassful of cooking oil! In total, a single kebab contains about 2,000 calories. Yowsers! There's no doubt that in general we're becoming a nation of couch potatoes, and more and more of us are way overweight. One guy I spoke to recently, a men's health specialist, said that in his opinion men are dying far too young as a result of their lifestyle choices.

So, today perhaps we should think about these verses and ponder the example we're setting to others around us. I have found that, rather than gorging, one of the best cures for stress or tiredness is a game of squash or a gentle jog round the block. I know that some of us may be disabled or suffering from long-term ill health but, whatever our circumstances, I think we can still honour God by respecting the bodies He has given us and trying to keep them as healthy as we can. And I don't mean just eating lentils ...

Prayer: I determine to try to get healthy and stay that way. Strengthen my resolve and make me an effective ambassador for Jesus through the way I live my life. Amen.

Gluttony is not a secret vice.
ORSON WELLES

57/Keep plugging away

'Do you not know that your bodies are temples of the Holy Spirit, who is in you, whom you have received from God? You are not your own; you were bought at a price. Therefore honour God with your bodies.' **1 Corinthians 6:19–20**

A few years ago now, I decided in a mad moment that before I turned 40 – my present age – I would run a marathon. There was a slight snag, however: I couldn't run more than a mile and I was slow. In fact, I was a bit concerned that I would be even slower than the bloke who did it one year in a Victorian diving suit. So the training started. At first, it seemed unachievable. I would run round the block and my calves would be killing me and I would be pouring with sweat. Gradually, however, I started to increase the distance, just a bit at a time. I began to try running up hills and slowly but surely I worked my way up to half-marathon standard. Along the way, I noticed that what I wanted to eat was changing and my clothes were getting looser. Eventually the big day came – and I nailed it. From a podgy bloke who couldn't run to a guy who ran a marathon without stopping took less than six months. Amazing, really, what a bit of self-discipline can do. There were times when I really didn't want to go running at all, but I hung in there and I got the prize.

Part of my motivation was a desire to be a better witness for Christ. I felt convicted that it was wrong to be unfit and a bit overweight. Ultimately, my body isn't only mine – I belong to Him. We may not all want to run a marathon, but let's all do *something*. Let us know on the Facebook page how you get on!

Prayer: I acknowledge that my body is a temple of the Holy Spirit. Inspire me to rise to the challenge and give me the self-discipline I need to get fit so that I can live well for You. Amen.

58/Beer o'clock

'Do not get drunk on wine, which leads to debauchery. Instead, be filled with the Spirit.' **Ephesians 5:18**

I've got some mates who are totally teetotal. In fact, my first ever boss in church work was strictly teetotal and he really challenged me to think about the whole issue. He used to say that if alcohol were discovered today it would probably be banned, it's so destructive to society! Some of my team at CVM have gone through periods of abstinence from time to time as a way to exercise self-discipline. Currently, one of them is not drinking anything for a year and he has really held the line. I think that's great!

Personally, I love a glass of wine and, while I'm not a massive beer or cider drinker, I can really appreciate a fine real ale or a vintage cider. I think the problems start to creep in, though, when you begin to look forward to that drink that you 'really need' just a bit too much or you find yourself saying, 'I could really use a beer!' I was speaking to one guy who told me that he and a few of his mates decided to write down how much they thought they were drinking and then record what they were actually consuming. They were amazed at just how much beer and wine they were chucking down their necks!

The biggest problem is when it starts to get a grip on you and begins to numb and blunt your relationship with the Holy Spirit. So, just a nudge of the conscience today to maybe wind it in a bit if we need to. If you've been looking forward to that beer or bottle of red just a bit too much lately, perhaps it's time to go on lime and soda for a while instead!

Prayer: Help me to live well for You and to be more dependent on You than on alcohol. Amen.

59/Workload

'There remains, then, a Sabbath-rest for the people of God; for anyone who enters God's rest also rests from their works, just as God did from his. Let us, therefore, make every effort to enter that rest, so that no one will perish by following their example of disobedience.'
Hebrews 4:9-11

I recently completed a two-week speaking tour. This came on top of leading an organisation and juggling all the hefty demands that go with such a job and even before it was over, I was exhausted. In fact, I was so tired towards the end that I managed to leave my laptop behind at one venue and drive 160 miles before I remembered! Not good at all.

So, when it came to finally downing tools, why did I feel guilty every time I put my feet up? When my wife and the kids were away in London for a few days, I even felt guilty putting on a DVD before

8pm. Madness, really. I had put a big shift in but still felt bad when I had a rest.

A lot of guys are like this but it's not healthy. It was only when I had dinner with an older and wiser Christian that something he said struck me deeply and helped to rejig my thinking. It was a throwaway line in between mouthfuls of pasta: 'Carl, you've got to learn to be kind to yourself ...'

So, there it is. We absolutely need to take proper rest and we've got to stop feeling guilty when we do. Learn to be kind to yourself and you'll probably be healthier and more productive as a result. And let me finish this thought by hitting, head on, the way we can be so mean to ourselves. I don't know where this comes from with Christians, but it's OK every so often to be generous to yourself as well as other people. It's when it gets out of balance and we become self-indulgent and greedy that there's a problem.

Prayer: Teach me the value of rest. Help me to be kinder to myself and to find a better balance between work and leisure. Amen.

60/Belly laugh

'A cheerful heart is good medicine, but a crushed spirit dries up the bones.' **Proverbs 17:22**

Here are some facts about laughing:

- The average pre-schooler laughs or smiles 400 times a day. That number will drop to only 15 times a day by the time he hits 35.

- People smile only 35% as much as they think they do.

- Laughter releases endorphins into the body, a chemical 10 times more powerful than the pain-relieving drug morphine. It has the same exhilarating effect as doing strenuous exercise.

- Every time you have a good hearty laugh, you burn up 3.5 calories.

There's a real epidemic of loneliness among men, and a lack of joy. Let me ask you a serious question: When was the last time you had a good laugh about something with your mates? The Bible is totally spot on. It's a fact that laughter is good medicine – God designed us with a sense of humour. So let me encourage you to make sure you do stuff on a regular basis that makes you crack up. Take time to watch some comedy. Keep company with people who make you laugh, not just people who take everything hugely seriously.

And don't take yourself too seriously, either. Far too many Christians are wound up too tightly. Take God's mission seriously, of course, and the things that are truly important, but don't lose the ability to laugh – and laugh at yourself. Be a man who puts a smile on other people's faces. There's a time for everything, so let's make more time for cracking up with our mates. How about, this Sunday, grabbing a few fellas and planning something fun? And, while you're at it, inviting a few mates along who don't know Jesus yet. Go get 'em!

Prayer: Bring people and situations into my life that make me laugh. And may I be a man who brings a smile to others as well. Amen.

THE MANUAL

More Bible notes for men written by Carl Beech.

Contain:

- 60 daily readings and prayers
- Two guest contributors
- Themes to encourage and challenge you

The Manual – Book 1:
Power/Poker/Pleasure/Pork Pies
ISBN: 978-1-85345-769-2

The Manual – Book 2:
Fighters/Keepers/Losers/Reapers
ISBN: 978-1-85345-770-8

The Manual – Book 3:
Son/See/Surf
ISBN: 978-1-85345-833-5

Also available in ebook formats